THAT TREE IS AMBITION

and other gems of life for all minds to treasure

by
Eulalio Abelgas

ISBNs:
eBook: 979-8-90224-001-3
Paperback: 979-8-90224-002-0
Hardback: 979-8-90224-003-7

Published by:
Authors Publishing House
178 Broadway, 3rd Floor, #1343
New York, NY 10001, USA

Main Line: (855) 624-0155
Email: support@authorspublishinghouse.com

Table of Contents

That Tree Is Ambition

I was up on a treetop
Where I was wont to be,
My world became bigger and wider
As far as the eyes can see.

And my grandpa would tell me
As he was wont to do:
"That tree is ambition,
The world is what there is to know."

"Climb your ambition to the top—
Accomplished, pure, and true;
And you just will not know it,
The world finds a successful you."

I listened, but heard him not.
Ambition is burden, the tree is fun;
They are two different things,
They could never be one.

Then I grew to be a grandpa,
Realized the wrongs I've done;
But there is no more recalling
Of the years wasted and gone.

Although, if we roll back all the years,
And care we take another look;
Another boy listened and took heed—
He builds bridges, writes many a book.

It is now, as before, clearly undebatable
That the tree symbolizes ambition;
And with so many trees around, pick one
That reminds you of your ambition.

Success Is Yours

Success is written across the sky
Each time a bird starts to fly,
Success is written across the field
When gardens are with fragrance filled.

Success is written in the wind
Each time a love bird finds a friend,
Success is written on every morn
That heralds a new creature born.

Never halfway, always full,
Success is the object of every goal;
And success is written on a person
When a goal is achieved and won.

But, success is not given, it is pursued,
A product of persevering attitude;
And success may be difficult or easy
Depending on one's mentality.

There is one simple secret though
That each young mind should ever know:
Success is easily achieved and won
If after the first step you keep going on.

3

When Duty Calls

The weeds are green, the reeds are tall,
I love them, I love them all.
They are pretty and they are wild,
Playmates of a carefree child;
They tickled me from side to side
When among them I crawled to hide;
I played among them through the sunshine
With full freedom that was mine.

But my love, my love cannot keep,
The plow from furrowing deep;
Turning over the green and tall,
Uprooting the weeds, reeds, and all.
Though among them I still love to hide,
In the field I cannot let them abide.
When duty calls, a friend may be lost
If it's for the good of all, or most.

Time to Win with Education

Time waits for no one!
Once it's gone, it's gone!
The best time to act, and how,
Is to take advantage of 'now.'

Although 'now', as present time, is narrow,
A thin line 'tween yesterday and tomorrow;
But no matter how small an arena for action,
It's enough to get a good education.

Education won't give you anything.
It only prepares you for anything.
And when you're prepared for anything,
Most likely you'll win many a thing.

With that kind of proposition,
Your best bet is good education.
This time, 'now,' take advantage,
Don't wait for your late old age.

Nothing to lose, many things to gain,
With the winners you will join,
When you pursue your life's ambition
With the help of good education.

The Right Choice

The school is only a building,
Cold and imposing from afar;
Yet within, it's warm and inviting
With the many warm people there are.

The prison is also a building,
A hostile building as had never been.
It is also inviting, although confusing,
With the violence and hatred therein.

Both buildings have knowledge to teach;
They're willing and eager if like you would.
The prison: usually, the road to evil is easy to reach.
The school: usually, it strives to teach only the good.

Which building would you rather go?
To a chaotic prison? Or to a lively school?
Here's a precious tip I can tell you:
To school goes the wise, to prison goes the fool.

The choice may be difficult or easy
Depending on your background;
But choose school, forget prison completely,
You'll live a life that is safe and sound.

The Caterpillar and the Butterfly

Once I looked at myself in the mirror,
I could not find what I was looking for;
And it dawned on me, a little thought,
I had not thought what I should find out.

Then I saw at the bottom of the mirror,
Crawling across was a caterpillar;
Undulating its way outside the window,
And rested on a leaf of a bush below.

Then, I watched from day to day,
To see what it might come to be;
For however small is a creature,
There's always a lesson from Nature.

And the once ugly caterpillar,
Became a cocoon of grim and horror;
Then emerged a magnificent butterfly,
A creature of beauty fluttering by.

And it dawned on me, a little thought,
How to realize the change I had sought;
I can change my ignorance to fortune,
If I pursue my ambition through education.

Champions All

Every person is a champion!
Emerging as the winner of the strife
Against all others in five hundred million,
A champion won the first race of life.

Then within the womb of nature,
A seed sprouted in incubation,
To be born at the destined hour
Into the world of the champion.

But the world is full of distractions
Which erode the qualities of a champion;
Human weaknesses and earthly temptations
Bring back the champion to oblivion.

To counter, human weaknesses can be fortified
With good character and conscience,
And earthly temptations can be nullified
By strong faith and prayerful solutions.

Then, oblivion will never be a threat.
A champion once can be champion again,
Making the second time around great,
Proving the first race was a glorious win.

The Peace Mender

I peeped through the eye of a needle,
And had a glimpse of eternity,
When I threaded a line thin and supple,
When it slid through as if endlessly.

Then I eyed the line for length
To see if it will serve the purpose,
And I tested the line for strength
If strong against the rigors of use.

Having satisfied the main requirement,
I had to proceed with my intention,
I had to work element by element,
Thorough to the culmination.

I proceeded to mend and sew
A tear, a rip, and any what for;
Whether big or small, whether old or new,
They looked like they weren't there before.

I also sewed to stick and attach
A button, a decor, or what have you;
Or I sewed on a decorative patch
To add colors to the life we knew.

Time came when I had to thread again
Another thin line through the needle,
When my eyes spotted in my brain
Reflections of different kinds of people.

Shown in states of chaos and disarray,
People of worldly misery to lofty grace;
I hope they can be sewn together someday
To nations having understanding and peace.

Stones

Stones here, there and everywhere.
They are as abundant as the air.
They come in myriads of sizes,
Reflecting the colors of the skies.

Stones they say are very old.
How old really I was not told;
But age doesn't matter anyway,
Like when it comes to you and me.

They have uses that we can't complain,
Like making the pots and pans shine;
Or white stones that powder easily,
Used to enhance a woman's beauty.

Stones are used in different ways
From high rise buildings to pathways,
Strong against the forces of nature
As they were built to really endure.

It is like a work of genius too,
To think the stones can be like you,
Having the attributes of the champions,
Strong character and lofty intentions.

People come and people go,
The stones stay and they're not few;
But stones always find a way
To give people places to stay.

People and stones associate everyday,
Each one's wares open for copy;
Just take care that as you grow on
You don't develop a heart of stone.

Humility

Has anybody seen the air?
Nobody! But it is just there!
Whether in dry lands devoid of rain,
Or the wet lands of forested mountain,
Even in places we have never been,
The air is there, though never seen.

It is unlike its cousin the wind
Whose furious storms men cannot bend,
But the air, in its gentle being—
Ever caressing, ever loving—
Does not need be seen while passing
Yet, ever so important, ever life-giving.

As a person grows in stature,
Be like the air in its humble nature,
Which chooses not to be seen
As it travels from glen to glen—
Ever life-giving, ever not forgetting—
Giving help is the important thing.

The Gift of Gratefulness

You can think or you can plan,
But if you don't move, nothing's done.
Whatever you want, whenever you can,
Actions give accomplishment to anyone.

A bird that simply sits on the branch
Gets no worm for its lunch.
A butterfly that doesn't flutter by
Becomes mateless under the sky.

The wind that simply sits still
Does not ruffle the daffodil.
The stone not thrown into the pool
Does not make the water ripple.

A journey planned but not taken
Is like a journey long forgotten.
A gratitude that is left unsaid
Makes a favor unappreciated.

However large or small the feat
There's always a place for credit;
Always maintain a sincere attitude
To express every bit of gratitude.

Bridges

Before you an endless river runs,
Separating you from lands of your desire;
But there are bridges—good and bad ones—
Choose well, avoid getting burned by fire.

Communication is the bridge to Understanding,
Making two minds share the same information,
Minimizing the chance of misunderstanding,
Ever cementing a harmonious relation.

Kindness is the bridge to Fulfillment,
Making helping others a pleasure,
A source of satisfaction, of merriment,
A showcase of a person's helpful nature.

Respect is the bridge to Warm Relationship,
Establishing the dominion of love,
Binding together a lasting friendship,
Everything fair: none below, none above.

Obedience is the bridge to Humility,
To Patience, Tolerance, and Endurance too.
Obedience leads to many places easily;
Obedience is one of the many bridges to go.

Violence is the bridge to Failure,
Leading to the world of the null and void,
Showing the nature of the evil creature;
Violence is the bridge to avoid.

Knowledge Is Power, but Beware

Knowledge comes to the observant,
To the one who sees and analyzes
The differences and the likenesses,
And the unquestionable outcome realizes.

Knowledge comes to the diligent in study,
Studying the proven works of others,
Amassing a wealth of knowledge
That could be a power of powers.

Knowledge is power. That is true!
But if stagnant in the mind, it is useless.
It can never be denied that
Knowledge unused is powerless.

It must be understood therefore that
Knowledge is power only when it is used,
But be cautioned that it is dangerous
When knowledge as power is abused.

Knowledge as power is dangerous
When imposed on helpless people,
When used to take advantage of
The weakness of unsuspecting people.

Rather, use knowledge as power
To benefit people who cling to hope,
By helping people find the strength
That give people the power to cope.

Humility Revisited

A flower vase on the table,

An empty container yet noble,

To contain a world of fragrance from a fragrant world.

Looking at it, many wonders before our eyes are unfurled:

Leaves of green hopes for a bright tomorrow;

Colors of life that our lives can borrow.

Looking at it, our thoughts fly to the land of dreams

Where thoughts slumber through sleepy streams.

Our thoughts fly far from where we are,

And see us in colors that are not what we are.

Yet, we find happiness and consolation

In such a temporary situation

Against the backdrop of eternity.

Then the sun wakes us up to reality,

And brings us to find in our universe,

Still on the table, a vase empty of flowers.

The Greatest Challenge

Behind your home is a mountain so high,
So high so that it seems to touch the sky,
Then you'll conquer that mountain over and over,
Until there is no more mountain to conquer.

Fronting your home spans the horizon and beyond,
So wide the expanse you can't see another land,
Then you'll conquer that expanse over and over,
Until there is no more expanse to conquer.

Beneath your home is a land so deep,
Holding treasures that took eons to keep,
Then you'll conquer the treasures over and over,
Until there are no more treasures to conquer

Above your home blankets the atmospheric air,
A vast domain of the creatures of the feather,
Then you'll conquer that vast domain of air,
Until there is no more airy dominion to conquer.

When the world and the universe are conquered all,
Inside your home you sit in the victory hall,
Staring at the poster that sits on a shelf,
"The greatest challenge is conquer your self."

The Measure of Success

Success is the object of every goal
That necessitates installing a control
To ensure that success is full and whole.

With success may come cheers and praises,
Applause, commendations, and bliss;
But these are not the measures of success.

Or it could be unending recognition,
Leading to undying jubilation,
Followed by continual celebration.

Or unblemished health it could be.
Or unlimited power fall where they may.
Or ever-growing wealth for all to see!

To some, with success comes fame,
Though not wanted it's part of the game,
Which through life may stick to a name.

But those are not the measures we seek.
Success is measured not by the fame or wealth you make,
But by how it's shared with the needy and the sick.

The Spices of Marriage

Two hearts met in a place so sweet,
Whispered words that hearts hold secret,
Until their two hearts closely entwined,
And in holy matrimony combined.

The years passed, as years never wait;
The two hearts are the same as they first met.
Two hearts separate from each other,
Divided by differences in personal character.

There is no need, though, for one to change the other,
For accepting one as one is, is much sweeter;
And the vows you made let no one put asunder,
Through sickness or in health, through richer or poorer.

Two different hearts can live a happy co-existence,
Sad on one's absence and glad in one's presence,
Tightening the knot with understanding and sacrifices
Which are considered life's greatest of spices.

Yes, happiness is available to contrasting twosome.
Although sacrifice is always difficult and irksome,
Just understand this principle and lavishly employ:
Love makes sacrifice easy; generous love makes it joy.

How I Love My Wife

It starts with meeting a complete stranger.

The following days come raining inspirations
Until a day witnesses a celebration
Of having a love that is accepted and reciprocated
By two hearts that beat as one.

The year before and the fifteen years after marriage
Is a collection of memories that I freeze in my mind
So that every time I look at my wife in the years thereafter,
I see a woman
At the zenith of her beauty and loveliness
Without the wrinkles of the ravages of Time;
For it helps living life
When we embrace the reality
That we don't stay young for always.

The early years mark the process of learning
That her snoring is music to my ears
Or that her nagging is a display of loving care.
Additionally, as hoped, and even expected,
The children come, filling some gaps in the relation,
Binding tightly the bond of marriage;
While comfortably knowing that when they grow up

The children follow the different paths of their ambition,
Leaving the parents to once again play house,
And the waiting game
Of when they may come to remember,
Or remember to come to visit;
And the meeting feels like the sunshine
Of a warm day in the season of Spring.

The middle years collect the wisdom
That nourishes the growth of each one's
Love, patience, and tolerance toward each other,
With the resolve never to abandon or abuse each other
In words and actions, in physical and mental,
In muffled emotions, or in silence.
We live as husband and wife, but most of all,
We are each other's best friends and playmates
As we play the game of married life.
We make moments of laughter rain every day,
And the bitter pills of life are all washed away
To the valley of rainbows
That brings back the living colors of happy days.

The later years map the journey
Towards the valley of life after life
With reminiscing of years gone by and life well-spent

From the beginning
Until the story is told.

And then…

It ends with a love that blooms forever.

To Florich, Anna Fleur, Niña Fleur, and Eurich

Constant thoughts of you
Water the seed of a tender feeling,
And from the garden of my heart
Bloom the flowers of love
That the hands of fervent prayers
Gently mold into a love song
That echoes forever.

I have but one life to live
In the silence of my loneliness.
I came to this world alone,
And I never expected
That I would need any companion.
When I first met you, however,
I could not imagine how to live
A life outside your world.
Thanks there is love to wrap two worlds
To a tight bundle of happiness,
And life delights in a never-ending dance
Of sunshine, rainbows and starlit fun.

You make me who I am;
With you by my side
Success is not far behind.
You give life to the flowers of love
Blooming in the garden of my heart,
And love nourishes the remembrance
Of my constant thoughts of you
That bloom eternally.

If not of your love and of our children's,
There would have been no life
For me to be proud of.

— Yours, Eulalio

Dedications to Friends in the Imaging Dept. and the EVS (2/28/2020)

Bailey:

> God wrote a poem,
>
> And His most beautiful poem by far
>
> Is the masterpiece that you are.

Dawn:

> Everyday dawn opens a new day;
>
> Every day you bring sunshine to my work day.

Karen B: Sheryl K:

> When lips are silent, the eyes talk,
>
> When feet stand still, the hearts take a walk;
>
> Beneath the stars and under the sun,
>
> Working with you was full of fun.

Tasha:

> Seeing your smile, hearing your laughter,
>
> Made my work a lot lighter.

Megan: (MRI)

> When you leave a warm "Good night,"

You tickle in me a child's delight.

Megan: Lizzy: Jennifer: Jessica: Becky A: (U/S)

    I never felt how hard I was working,

    'Cuz you made me feel I was only playing.

Michele: Nichole: Connie: John:
Dustin: Donald: Jordan: Craig: (C/T)

    It is the thought that matters,

    It makes strangers like brothers and sisters.

Sarah:

    While flowers in the garden bloom,

    You share your fragrance in the work room.

Karla:

    Your heart is to everyone's desire,

    It rained pain when time to retire.

Greg: Tronie: Royal: Lucy: Shelly: Dustin: Connie: Roger: Sheryl:
Laura: Frankie: Mike: Jasmin: Ken: Chris: Others:
(EVS; 2009-2020)

    Names of many friends have escaped remembering,

    But the friendship with all of you is beyond forgetting.

                          — Yours, Lee

The Best Bridge

A bridge connects one to another,
It connects the here to the yonder;
And no matter where you are,
It makes near that which is far.

A bridge spans across the troubled water
Of a surging stream or a raging river,
So that you can transport with ease
That which would have been otherwise.

Or a bridge can connect two persons,
Who would have been of different opinions;
Weld a friendship that is warm and lasting,
Or even create a lifelong understanding.

All the bridges described thus far
Are as good bridges as there are,
But the best of bridges ever
Are hands busy helping another.

Make Your Mark

Life is a journey
To a land far away;
Your sojourn here's temporary,
What will mark your stay?

Time flits, and so is life,
At the ticking of a clock;
The trudging is ever onward,
There is no turning back.

Fortunes come and fortunes go
While on a lifelong quest
For the mark to mark your stay
Before you lay down to rest.

Footprints can be erased by time,
Memories can forget a name,
Monuments are blown to dust,
And fame is just a passing game.

But carve your name in the hearts of people
With a good deed that betters your best,
Then you have a mark that marks your stay;
It may be the last, but surely not the least.

On Drug Addiction: As I Am

Finally I saw the paradise of drug addiction
When I took a shot and carefree-ly dreamed on
In imagined happy colors that colored my happiness.
Oh, what a thrill! It tickled my consciousness!

But once was not enough; I had to take 'one more.'
Oh, the thrill, it was higher than before!
And the 'one more' happened again and again
Until I felt no more joy—only the pain.

There was this chronic pain of an unknown illness
That was acutely eroding my basal happiness,
When I was conscious and fully awake,
When I was sober and not on the take.

'Twas very frustrating, like caught in a quicksand;
Escape was impossible though escape was at hand.
I hoped I could escape by another form,
Even if like waking up from a bad storm.

Progressively it became an obsessive task
To make a question and proceed to ask:
Shall I remain like Pinocchio, the puppet toy,
Or alive in life as a real grown up boy?

How I hoped there was a surefire way
To rescue this suffering poor old me
From this deceitful hell of drug addiction
And back to a normal living condition.

Finally, I woke up in a rehab center,
Which seemed far although really near;
Then, I submitted myself to rehabilitation,
And got all the help I could count on.

Drug addiction is now a thing of my past.
I am now cleansed and drug-free at last.
Drug addiction, I say, is a thrill not worth a try;
Whoever says it is, is telling a big lie.

On Drug Addiction: As They Are

I see some people with vibrant energy
Slink into a kind of narcotic lethargy,
And others successful in chosen career
Lose direction, stumble and falter.

I see some religious and pious people
Forsake the messages of the Bible,
And lives of members of happy families
Turn into gruesome or fatal tragedies.

Even common people are affected too
When to alcohol and drugs they go;
Allowing themselves to wallow in prison
In the world of addiction and perdition.

Addiction is a very selfish vice.
It is unhealthy and never nice.
Even worse than a vice it's a disease
That makes a person's world to cease.

Sometimes there is a time to be unsure,
But for those who choose, there is a cure;
And for those who have finally decided,
It really pays to be rehabilitated.

A new life is a triumphant rebirth
Of the old life of glory and mirth,
When you commit to rehabilitation,
And you stay away from addiction.

But whatever the success or gain,
It will simply turn to bitter pain,
If you return to your addicted state,
And seal your life in a sordid fate.

Then, all those years of doing the best,
All those years simply go to waste,
All for the woeful and worthless reason:
The scourge of alcohol and/or drug addiction.

On Drug Addiction: As You and I

There are people who are easily affected
When they are lonely and feeling neglected;
They feel helpless, hopeless, and ego down,
Though at the center of a bustling town.

There are people who have feelings of guilt,
Whether of real or just imagined guilt;
They can only think of escaping the situation
By resorting to alcohol and/or drug addiction.

Addiction, at best, is a short-term cure,
At worst, it's a lifetime curse to endure;
And you are drowned in a losing supposition—
Anchored deep in alcohol and/or drug addiction.

When Misfortune deals you an overdose,
Your life story comes to a tragic close;
Angels can't bring you back to life again,
Friends and relatives are left in grieving pain.

There are many reasons to resort to drugs,
Yet, many reasons too not to turn to drugs;
All you need is a strong personal conviction
To avoid all and every call of temptation.

While some can do it on their own,
Others are weak when they are all alone;
Seek good friends—they help in every front—
Whether you know it or whether you don't.

There are the bold and there are the meek,
There are the strong and there are the weak;
But whoe'er you are among the persons,
Live a life of godly propositions.

On Drug Addiction: The Drug Pusher

Drug addiction happens because the user
Yielded to the enticements by the pusher
Who has everything that his trade could offer
In order to add to his list another number.

Drug pushing is part of a business syndicate
That relies on the pushers on the street
To peddle the merchandise to the customers
Who are the users and other pushers.

The pusher links the user to the organization
That baits the pusher with a big compensation
Regardless of the ruin of the user's character
That is killed in a manner worse than murder.

Yes, there is big money in drug pushing.
To the impoverished it is very tempting;
But to the law, drug pushing is a crime,
When you're caught, you must serve time.

Although the pusher is rich in money,
A pusher's life is really not that easy.
In the criminal world there are many predators
That are worse than the hyenas and the vultures.

Yet drug pushing is not all about money.
It's also about the pusher's loss of empathy,
Mercilessly preying on his fellow human being,
Reducing himself to a satanic parasitic thing.

If only the pusher recognizes that the user
Is similarly the pusher's sister or brother
Whose life he must not expose to peril;
It is then time to unmask the devil!

So, users and pushers, open your eyes;
Look and find the truth behind the lies:
The road to addiction is not paved with gold.
The wares of drug pushing you put on hold.

From Small Deeds to Great Pride

A man once looked for great things to be done.
He searched the world wherever he can,
But he could not find any the Almighty had not done,
So he thought there's nothing left to be done by man.

A sage he met one day said: "Give me your trust.
The high mountain Everest is simply made of dust;
The most beautiful beach is made of fine sand;
A drop of water the ocean; a pinch of sod the land."

"All great things are made up of little things,
They abound around us like rings;
There is no need to look far and wide,
From little things there is no place to hide."

And so the man looked not so far around,
And picked a piece of garbage off the ground,
Helped an old woman cross a crowded street,
And all these things made him feel great.

Yes, there is no need to look far and wide.
Little things can still be sources of pride.
A little bit of honesty, a little bit of kindness,
A little bit of trust for a world of peace.

How to Handle Success

Success can be like a drink, so intoxicating
That it makes a person forget his beginning.
He remembers the tree but not the seed,
And forgets those who helped him succeed.

When such a story do come to happen,
That person's success was won in vain;
All the victories of all the battles fought,
All mean nothing, and they come to naught.

He becomes the hunter caught in his trap,
Alone in the woods with nary a nap,
Even with a crowd milling around,
Not one help, only worms on the ground.

That is the danger lurking ahead
For those who put success in the head;
They become stone drunk and blinded,
And success brings failure indeed.

When success comes, make it like a wand,
Under your control at the flick of a hand;
Humbly point to the object of your quest,
And win the object through a humble request.

Let Freedom Reign

Freedom is a very sacred thing;
It can make you a Queen or King.
Though there's one thing to remember:
You are your own king, not of another.

Freedom can be a given or a riddle
Operating with this one principle:
You are free to think of anything,
But not free to do everything.

You are free to give everything you have,
But not free to take everything you love.
If you breach another's freedom in what you do,
For your actions you will answer to the law.

Is freedom limited by the law of the land?
No and never. They go hand in hand.
For your power to rule your kingdom,
freedom provides.
For wisdom so you don't trespass another's
kingdom, the law guides.

Freedom is not without limitation;
It started from the time of Creation.
Adam was free to eat all that can be eaten,
But not from the tree at the center of Eden.

Freedom defines the borders of your kingdom,
The law defines the exclusions of your freedom;
Wherever you look, wherever you go,
No person ever is above the law.

To accept that every person has freedom is wise,
And to deny that fact is the most unwise.
So, live with the truth and be happy,
And everyone is peaceful and merry.

The Grass on the Battlefield

Men without consideration,
Even without my invitation
You are invading my turf at your discretion.

The weight of your boots
Have bent my stalks to the ground
And worn out the greenness of my life.
Slowly but surely my body is turning
To the sick yellow and the dead brown.
Your war is ramming down my throat
What I cannot easily relish!
Long have I roiled under your intrusion,
Long have I suffered under your aggression.

Although, one thing is consoling:
That after the last gun had silenced,
And the last smoke of war had wafted away,
There will I be,
Standing proud and tall
Over the mound that covers you.

Ships of Decision

A ship is safe and sound in the harbor,
But that is not what ships are made for;
It was made as a vessel to carry the braves
As it crashes through and rides over the waves.

A ship is not meant to sleep on calm water,
But awake and alive battling bad weather;
As it brings all the bold and spirited braves
Across the oceans and over the waves.

Had it not been for ships and men of brawn,
There wouldn't have been new knowledge won,
Nor new continents discovered and scored,
If the ships were forever safely moored.

So learn a lesson from the ship and the men,
Who know when a risk is well-taken,
Conquer your undecided self from within,
There's nothing to lose, good things to gain.

Formula for Success

Good luck is a help in any endeavor,
But it is not available every hour;
You don't know where it is coming from,
You don't know when it will come.

Inspiration is another helpful commodity,
But the same, it's not available every day.
And when it comes, does it come to stay?
Or does it swiftly fly away?

Opportunity is the good reason
Why you need good luck and inspiration;
But making the three ingredients meet
May take forever if you just wait.

Their joint availability is an uncertainty,
And waiting for them may take eternity;
Waiting and waiting are a waste of time,
And you end already past your prime.

So, while you are young and able,
Make the three ingredients available;
Make opportunity, good luck, and inspiration
By your own hard work and determination.

46

Hard work will heat up the iron from cold
So that the iron will be easy to mold;
And you can mold it to any fashion
By your own hard work and determination.

Plan for Accidents

The future cannot be prevented from coming,
But future accidents can be prevented from happening.
Now, that may be easier said than done,
But when you're determined to do it, you can.

An accident is an untoward incident
Which spoils the success of a great event.
So, when you embark on an endeavor,
Plan accidents to happen therefor.

There is no substitute for good planning
So that you know what is coming,
And an ounce of preparation today
Can prevent a pound of cure someday.

Accidents don't just happen, they're allowed to happen,
Or ignored and hoped not to come to happen;
But accidents happen when least expected
To those who are the worst affected.

Avoiding accidents is not a game of chance.
It's a deliberate effort before any performance
By identifying the word-for-word definition
Of the step-by-step process of the operation.

Then one-by-one question, probe or examine
For whatever wrong may come to happen
On the what, where, when, why, and how.
Then you can prevent what you know.

When prepared, you won't be taken aback,
And there is no need to blame bad luck.
An accident-free performance is a success,
And it bodes well for further progress.

The Tenses in Life

If you are not, I'll make you familiar
With the simple tenses of grammar;
The past, present, and future of be,
Like the were, are, and shall or will be.

As you travel through the sea of lives,
You could be the one who really strives
To improve your present position,
And be better than the other person.

When it happens, and sure it will,
Because of your determination and will;
Don't forget the people you left behind,
They need help from a person of your kind.

And in giving help, put it not in future tense,
But rather, in the past and present tense;
Because a promise made for a future
Is usually doomed to forgetting and failure.

The past and present accomplishments sound
Better than any promises still future bound,
And there is no tune that sounds better than
Calling who had been helped one by one.

Give Love to Old Mother Dear

I see my old guitar tucked in the corner.

Looking at her,

my memory brings me back

to the hallways of the past.

I see a boy with his arms

wrapped around her waist,

his little fingers caressing

the strings of her heart.

And I hear the strains of a lullaby

that many times before

lulled me to sleep

in the warm safety on her lap.

Looking at her,

I remember I tucked her there years ago.

When I grew in age,

I found different diversions in life

that took me away from the pleasures

of playing with my guitar.

So now,

she sits in a corner cold and damp.

Her body and face

all cracked and wrinkled from disuse,

crooked in pain from neglect,

slowly collecting the dust of anonymity.

Seeing her now,
a compelling feeling takes me near her.
And I touch her.
And I caress the strings of her heart.
And the lullabies begin to flow from her bosom
as they had flowed abundantly before.

But the lyrics are different and strange
as they run this way
in muffled agony:
"Long have I yearned for you to touch me,
caress me.
Long has my voice remained unheard.
Long have I wanted to sing you a lullaby
before I die."

Two Views of a Woman

Gracious and fair to the eyes,

Fairer than the rainbow in the skies,

Fragrant blossom of loveliness,

Warm comfort in loneliness,

A pillar of strength to lean on,

A sweet and steadfast companion,

A fountain of all the pleasures proved,

A person not to be hurt but loved.

Early bird of the early morn,

Gentle nurse when a child is born,

Patient teacher of the first flight,

Treasure chest of a child's delight,

The lullaby that rocks the cradle,

The guiding light till a child is able,

The co-maker at a child's birth,

The guardian angel here on earth.

To a husband: a woman is a friend and wife;

To a child: a woman is a mother and life.

When the two views are rolled into one,

Great is man's love for the woman,

For love that's borne by a child's innocence

Carries no pain or any mark of violence.

Then spouses will be bound tighter when
Living with bliss that's made in Heaven.

Respect Is Ever Due

Too often, from many persons we hear,
That respect is earned, and given never.
Is it that way since the distant past,
Or a new notion that is made to last?

Could it be also that there are respects
That depend on what a person expects?
Because, we hear exhortations of respecting
Nature, the Earth, animals, or even a thing.

Respect, to be required to be earned,
May be true for skills that are learned;
But there is always a respect for a person
Just because a person is a person.

The Creator made a noble creation
In the form of a respectable person,
Who has the power to rule the Earth
Ever since the Biblical first birth.

It is true, nothing and nobody is perfect,
But every person deserves his/her due respect;
Because, whatever is his/her imperfection,
Doesn't make him/her less of a person.

Open the Paths to Success

To say "Get an education" is easy.
To say "I'll get an education" is also easy.
But in the actual measure of a life's run,
Such statements are easier said than done.

Nowadays, education is very costly,
Out of reach for people in poverty;
But that is if you bow down and buckle,
Rather than strive to fight or struggle.

For an escape from your misery,
Take a lesson from a real life story
Of a man who had very less to spend,
But who was very successful in the end.

Wearing nothing but homespun clothes,
We may see the ill fortune it forebodes;
But there is no telling, because his ambition
He pursued with dogged determination.

Studying comfortably in any nooks,
Spending much of his time on borrowed books;
Even with playing games and many a diversion,
He let nothing affect his concentration.

After his studies he traveled far,
Took an examination and passed the bar,
Became one of the brilliant politicians,
And became a President of the Americans.

Find your course and pursue it
Through work scholarship or through debt;
Just remember that after your studies
Are laid open the paths to success.

Then, as a successful parent of a family,
Or successful member of a community,
Remember that in everything you do
There is an Abraham Lincoln in you.

Save the Planet Earth

This is the one and only planet Earth,
The one and only place of my birth;
If it succumbs to the abuses that people do,
There's no other planet for me to go to.

Scientists are looking for home planets to-be,
Which could be zillions of lightyears away;
With my life span of less than a hundred years,
Exoplanet is no solution to my fears.

This is my one and only planet Earth,
Silent witness to my sorrow and mirth; I
may work at climate change obviation,
But I can't do all of them all alone.

I need help from all of Earth's population,
Counting from those who cause all the pollution,
Up to the effective, down to the doubtful ones,
And positive actions from politicians.

But this climate change we're talking about
Has many of you still beclouded with doubt.
The reason: Climate change may not be true.
You're not thinking: What if it is true?

It is not I alone who calls Earth home;
You, too, and your generations to come.
So, can't we just be the do-gooders
Rather than the numb unthinking deniers?

Time may be running out on everyone.
It may not be if but when is global extinction.
When the fateful date reaches me and you,
None will be left to say, "I told you so."

Listen to the Voice of a Tough Guy

I am a violent child.
I live a life carefree and wild.
I am the king of my brood,
My kingdom is the road!

Advices of my folks I do not hear;
They can only cringe in fear.
There's no better than I to rule
The kingdom of the cruel!

You can look for me whence
There is a rumble of violence;
That can be any street corner.
Surely, you will find me there!

But at quite a young age
I left that violent stage.
I breathed my last breath
At my early violent death.

On Bullying: The Parents and the Bully

As no person is born holy,
So is no person born a bully,
But when a bully shows at personhood,
Someone didn't do something good.

A child reared in the wild by a wolf
Acquires the characteristics of that wolf.
In real life, that wolf represents
No other than the child's parents.

The parents are the child's teachers
Of the good morals that Faith offers,
And what the parents have observed,
Or what the parents have absorbed.

But how can such parents teach the child,
If the parents live their lives beguiled:
Could be cheating, or love lost its force,
Hard to please, quarrelsome, or quick to divorce.

The hands that ought to hold the child are gone.

The hearts that ought to teach the child are gone.

Negligence overwhelms the role of responsibility,

Dereliction of duty clearly comes into play.

If you want to be the parents of a child,

You teach him not to be violent or wild,

Teach him love and respect for every person,

Teach him to practice charity and compassion.

Then, as parents, hold on to your Faith,

And hold a prayer in your every breath.

Parenting, however done, isn't light and easy;

Though the burdens are fun, they are heavy.

On Bullying: Suicide Is Not an Option

Our lives have never been our own.
They are with us only as a loan.
We're not even empowered to return them;
It's up to the Maker when He takes them.

True, sometimes living becomes so tedious
So that snuffing out one's life seems ingenious,
But when you choose to wake up every morn,
That's one way everyday heroes are born.

A life lived to see another day is bravery,
A life clipped to end the day is cowardly;
There's no braver act than to face the changes
Resulting from life's unannounced challenges.

Likewise, no amount of bullying, or any reason,
Should change the course that your life is on.
The child that you are, beautiful and smart,
Deserves no less than a throbbing living heart.

Not even a life lived in constant fear
Of what today and tomorrow might bear
Will justify doing the detestable action,
Which, in the first place, is not your option.

Just think of all the sunshine wrapped in joy,
All the kin and friends bringing life's buoy,
And new dance steps to the songs of minstrels
Bringing on life's attendant kicks and thrills.

It is not you alone you will save,
You will save also those who will grieve,
For even if an island seems a solitary one,
It's really not alone. You, too, are not alone.

May this presentation help you decide
That there's no glory in any form of suicide;
A life lived fully is still better to have
Than an untimely trip to the grave.

On Bullying: The Bully

He finds joy in the distress of others
To build a cover for his inner fears
That he will find the truth one day
That lonely is the world of a bully.

So he melds a crowd around him,
And he continually entertains them
By bullying others outside the cult
Whether with or without any fault.

When you meet a bully on your path,
Give him your pity not your wrath;
It's for the sane to be loving and kind,
For within, a bully's sick in his mind.

And may the bully see in him
The notoriety, not the fame;
For making another person miserable
Is neither blessed nor noble.

It must be realized, therefore,
Whatever the kind of measure,
There's never an ounce of good
In a billion tons of bullyhood.

There's only for the bully to realize
To follow the lead of the wise:
To hold the tongue that lashes out,
To stay the hands that flail about.

To survey through the eyes of a dove,
And give everyone a chance for love;
Then we'll find a billion tons of good,
And never an ounce of bullyhood.

Doors

Doors, doors, and many more doors
Concealing secrets behind closed doors;
But many doors betray the character
Of whoever is living in there.

The doors stand proud and still,
Portrait of a dutiful sentinel;
Or they show nothing and left bare
By the owners who seem not to care.

There are doors that show the stance
Sustaining the face of arrogance,
Although doors are easy to open
To welcome a weary stranger in.

A philosophy in life I learned
From the doors of which I yearned:
It is easier to give sight to the blind
Than open the door of a closed mind.

The beauty of the doors show
Under the shimmer of angel glow
As the inky dark of the night
Is decked with the twinkling starlight.

The hidden beauty of the doors though
Are what secrets there are to know,
Which give my mind fanciful flights,
Which give me many sleepless nights.

In my desire to enter many doors
Which may or may not welcome visitors,
I realize, I have almost forgotten
The beacon of the door to Heaven.

Dreams

Dream big and dream deep
While you're awake or in your sleep,
For dreams can take you away
To places where minds work and play.

The wakeful dreams can better say
The meaningful opinions of the day,
While the dreams in inspired sleep
May bring inventions to use and keep.

Dreams can make many possibilities
For imaginations to become realities,
And realize the useful tools of mankind
As machineries are harvested from the mind.

A dream starts the journey of ambition
Towards the sought-after good fortune,
But along the way walk with diligence
Prodded by perseverance and patience.

For the road is long and winding,
And the destination seems not looming;
Yet when the long journey is done
The sweat and perspiration are also gone.

When a friend tells you his dream,
Keep the subject in a burning flame,
So that the meaning is retained,
And not forgotten in the end.

If the message is important to you,
Make the dream your dream too;
It will be easy to adopt that way,
For it will have your own identity.

If it remains a dream you've heard,
It remains with the things absurd;
Whether it was oral or written,
It can be thrown away and forgotten.

At first glance dreams may look insignificant,
A second look may spot something important;
The common rule is intelligent sorting,
Concluded with informed critical thinking.

Look There — a Man

Hangs there a man on the cross.
Who is he? Nobody knows!
He looks like any common person,
Anonymous among fellow creation.

Some people have strayed far away
From that time on the crucifixion day;
Time which might have been long enough
To forget the Giver of our stuff.

Though their world is the world we dwell,
The people might have changed quite well,
Thus, memories seem to have forgotten
That our final destination is Heaven.

Love and compassion Heaven teaches us,
Some politicians reject without a blush;
Some even act like denizens of hell
When they live their lives full of evil.

God teaches people to love their enemies,
But politicians choose vengeance for their enemies;
With that they claim they are doing the best,
But godly people know some politicians are beast.

Some politicians seem to have axes to grind
When colleagues they treat so unkind,
And some politicians behave like fools
When in them greed for power rules.

And the lord of the ring of liars
Is enabled by his horde of dirty liars;
They tempted many of the credulous
By feigning as deeply religious.

No wonder some people have forgotten
That our final destination is Heaven;
Some people are hopelessly that bad
To forget the merciful and loving God.

So, don't hang the voters on the cross,
Instead, free them of their dreaded woes;
In your time, choose to be the true statesman—
Not a lying, selfish, vengeful politician.

What Went Wrong

Truth is very rarely ever found
In today's bum political ground;
When a politician says something,
More often than not—he is lying.

When this nation was in its infancy,
The people enjoyed true democracy,
The politicians gave unselfish service,
The people had few to complain of malice.

Comparing ere and today's politicians all,
Poor service causes the people's downfall,
The people's aspirations ignored or brushed aside,
The politicians' and the people's interests collide.

This country united has its people divided
According to each political party's creed;
The people allowed wrongly the political party
To dictate to the people their destiny.

Don't choose to be a democrat or republican,
Choose higher—remain the true American;
Don't let the political parties choose you,
You choose the politicians to work for you.

Why choose one of less stature and flat
When you can be much better than that?
Why choose to be a democrat or republican
When you can remain the honorable American?

When "We the People" assert their sovereignty,
You can be assured of your esteem and dignity;
You don't have to beg from any politician,
You remain the free and sovereign American.

Then teach the politicians to value truth for the people
So they can regain their self-worth to the people,
For they are nothing without the sovereign people
As their power comes from the sovereign people.

The Statesman and the Politician

When you have become the success
That you wanted to be,
You may want to join to play
In the playground of the rich
In the realm of politics.

But before you join politics
Know the distinction
Between the two entities:
The Statesman and the Politician.

A Statesman[1] is a person
Who shows wisdom and skill
In conducting state affairs
And treating public issues,
Or one experienced or engaged
In the business of government.
When you can work bi-partisan-ly
With cooperation and compromise
For the attainment of the people's aspirations;
When you work in an able, far-seeing,
Principled conduct of public affairs;

When you hunger for service
To improve the people's lives on the aspects
Of health, wealth, safety, and peace
Above your own interests;
You have the qualities of a Statesman
And you are invited to play
In the playground of politics.

A Politician[1] is a person
Who is actively engaged in politics,
Especially party politics,
With implications of seeking
Personal or partisan gain,
Scheming, opportunism, etc.
When you are a hard party-liner
Who cannot cooperate and compromise
With the other political party members
For the good of the people;

---

[1] Definitions taken from Webster's New World Dictionary of the American Language, College Edition, Copyright 1960.

When the people's aspirations
Have no importance to you;
And when you hunger for political power
For yourself against the wishes of the people;
You have the mark of a Politician.
You may not be invited there,
Although you can invite yourself.

The choice is either a Statesman
Or a Politician, there's no hybrid.
If you choose to be a Statesman
It's a wow to the people;
If you choose to be a Politician
It's woe to the people.

Your Life

Your life is just as good as the body that harbors it.
Yes, you can live in years of glory,
Even live in the ecstatic psychology of hope,
But at the end of the day,
Your life will mirror the pain that your body feels.

It is important to note that it is usually at old age
That the body feels the pain caused by the neglect and abuses
That were absorbed and ignored by the body in its youth.
It is important to note, again,
That a body well taken care of when young
Will ripen to a good life at old age.

Taking care of the body starts with giving it
The macronutrients of carbohydrates, proteins, and fats,
And the micronutrients of vitamins and minerals
In grains, meats, vegetables and fruits
In a balanced diet of multi-colors.
As your body ages,
Its efficiency in absorbing nutrients diminishes in time;
It is important that you start right in your youth.

Among the macronutrients,
Carbohydrates is nearly 100 percent converted
To sugar, in addition to sugar itself,
To supply the body with the energy
That moves the muscles, fuels the brain,
And helps promote good digestive health.
Examples of sources of carbohydrates are
Starchy foods, fruits and vegetables,
Legumes, whole grain, cereal, tubers, milk.

Proteins in the blood help fight infections,
Build and repair body tissues,
Effect biochemical reactions related to
Energy production, growth, digestion,
Muscle function and blood clotting.
Among the sources of proteins are
Fatty fish, red and white meat,
Cheese variety, animal milk, legume,
Green, white, red and yellow vegetables.

Fats are for giving the body energy,
Supporting cell growth, protecting organs,
And helping the body absorb vital nutrients.
Sources of fats are fatty acids omega 3 and 6
Which come mostly from hemp seeds,

Edamame beans, chia seeds, and salmon;
Monounsaturated fats coming from
Avocado, pistachio, peanut butter, extra
Virgin olive oil, almonds, or olives;
Polyunsaturated fats such as tofu;
And saturated fats from whole eggs,
Plain whole milk Greek yogurt,
Or red and white animal meat.

The fats you eat are converted to cholesterol.
Cholesterol is a fat-like substance
Found in all of your cells, produced by the liver,
To help keep cells from breaking down;
Cholesterol is also involved in the production
Of hormones and vitamins.

It's good to know there are good and bad cholesterols.
LDL (low-density lipoprotein), the bad cholesterol,
Builds up plaques in arteries, can risk heart disease;
Often found in red and white meat, dairy products,
Coconut oils and some fried or baked foods.
VLDL (very low-density lipoprotein), bad cholesterol,
The primary ride for triglycerides in the blood.
HDL (high-density lipoprotein), the good cholesterol,
Helps remove cholesterol from the arteries,

Returns them to the liver for disposal in the stool;
Often found in seeds, nuts, beans and salmons.
Triglycerides are types of cholesterol found in the blood,
Bad cholesterol, also increases the risk of heart disease;
Stored in fat cells and released for energy between meals,
Most abundant type of cholesterol in your body;
Levels of triglyceride are raised by
Primarily eating foods that are high in
Added sugar, saturated fat, drinking too much alcohol,
And especially, consuming fats like butter and oil.
Total Cholesterol, the total amount of cholesterol in blood,
It includes the LDL, VLDL, HDL and triglycerides.
Non-HDL Cholesterol, is the Total Cholesterol
Minus the HDL (good cholesterol),
Is the measure of bad cholesterol in your blood.

Cholesterol circulates throughout the body
With the bloodstream, and when it has too much LDL,
It can form plaques on the walls of blood vessels,
Narrows the blood vessel and block
The healthy flow of blood in the body,
And may cause heart attack or other problems.

All the nutrients will be processed internally
By a healthy body for the health of the body,
And this health of the body is enhanced
By eight hours of sleep each night to recharge your system,
By a serene spirit free of anger, envy and hate,
By quitting the bad habit of alcoholism and smoking,
By not engaging in illegal drugs addiction,
By excluding the world of the germs and viruses
Through washing the hands in not less than fifteen seconds
Every time you touch dirt, when doubtful, and before eating.

Eating can make you healthy,
But what you eat may make you sick.
Most of the foods carry substances that turn to sugar.
Sugar is converted by the body into energy
To move the muscles to make the body work,
And sugar is the brain's main fuel.
At the right quantity, food is the elixir of health;
At excess, food is poison to the body.
The key word is moderation, and
Don't exceed what is recommended.

For good performance of your body
Make it a habit of seeing a health provider regularly,
When you are also healthy, not just when you are sick.

Watch Out for Two Killer Foods

Sugar and table salt are the two foods
You should watch out for.
In right quantities
Both foods make the foods you eat
Palatable and acceptable to the taste buds.
Moreover, sugar is the source of energy
That makes the muscles do work,
And it is the primary food of the brain.

Blood sugar is what is meant
By the term glucose.
The glucose in your body
Comes from three macronutrients:
About 10 percent of the fat,
About 50 percent of the protein,
And nearly 100 percent of the carbohydrate
Is turned to sugar,
In addition to the simple sugar you ingest.

In a healthy person,
Glucose level between meals ranges
From 70 to 99 milligrams per deciliter (mg/dl).
When fasting glucose level is more
Than 125 mg/dl in two consecutive occasions,

Diabetes is diagnosed.

A person may not die of diabetes itself,
But from the complications thereof.
In uncontrolled diabetes,
The glucose level becomes toxic to the body,
Blood thickens and difficult to flow through
The blood vessels, especially the capillaries,
Starving the affected body parts and organs
Of the needed nutrients and oxygen,
And severe damage occur
In your eyes, kidneys, feet, and heart.
The eyes can be blinded.
The feet can be amputated.
The kidneys and heart can fail.
Kidneys on the way to failure
Cause high blood pressure
Which overworks the heart;
High blood pressure in turn
Aggravates the bad condition of the kidneys;
And the cycle continues in a vicious circle
Causing either the kidneys or heart to fail.
A failed heart transfers your residence
To six feet under the ground
With no more cellphone services.

Failed kidneys require that you undergo dialysis procedure
To cleanse the accumulated toxins off your blood
At least three hours per day, three days per week,
Until you get kidney transplant or die.

Table salt is largely composed of
Sodium and chloride.

Sodium is involved in muscle contraction, heartbeat,
Nerve impulses and conduction;
And digestion of body-building protein.

Chloride preserves acid-base balance in body;
Aids in absorption of potassium which is
Needed for normal heart and muscle action;
And enhances the ability of blood to carry
Carbon dioxide from respiring tissues to the lungs.

In right quantity, salt is essential in aiding the kidneys
In its important function of hydration of the body.
In excess quantity, salt can cause high blood pressure,
Aggravate the bad condition of the kidneys ;
In low quantity, hyponatremia may cause death
In old folks, which is also caused by illnesses such as
Kidney disease, heart disease, liver failure, diabetes,

Or excessive drinking of water during physical activities
Which effects lowering the number of salt per
Liter of water in the body (known as hyponatremia);
Or impaired fetal development in pregnant women.

For your best of health, see a doctor regularly;
Quit the bad habits of smoking and alcoholism
Which affect negatively many body functions;
Never try or get hooked to addictive drugs.
Maintain normal blood pressure, blood lipids (fats),
Check regularly body weight (or body mass index);
And engage in proper physical exercise at a time
When the heart and body are able and ready
To welcome such activities.
You start doing these things for your benefit
When you are young and healthy, and
After consultation with your health care provider.

Before It Is Too Late

With my years on Earth reaching eighty,
I could say that it is too late for me;
It is too late for me to realize
That I lived my life with closed eyes.

It does not mean that I walked blind,
I spent my consciousness with open mind;
But because of living in carefree abandon, I
squandered my health for no good reason!

I spent my youth in chasing ambition,
Which, with my diligence, I easily won;
But I forgot that sometimes successes
Can trigger unwelcome carelessness.

I basked under the delusion of success,
The doctors' appointments I cared less;
When I was young I was stubborn and strong,
Recognizing errors took time too long!

I indulged freely in foods that cause
High blood pressure and high blood glucose;
And most of the other illnesses,
Showed after I had diabetes.

I did not follow well the doctors' advices
Which were meant for my body's wellness.
I thought with determination and will,
I could keep my body hale and stay well.

At the age of eighty I'm at my achy years,
Achy body and eyes pooling with tears.
No more time to correct my errors,
May there be time to advise others.

I'm reaching out to the youths of today
Who still have healthy years and a day;
While you're young you're at your best prime,
See a doctor for your healthy clime.

As for me, my life has one consolation:
A close-knit family hitched in happy union,
Beyond the place where my Sun is set,
To where our Maker and we will meet.

Behind the Obvious

The Sun rises in the east.
That is the fact. That is the accepted truth.
But you may not believe me when I say
It's not true that the Sun rises in the east.

Based on science, between the Sun and the Earth,
The Sun is fixed on its place in space,
While it is the Earth that rotates on its axis
And revolves around the Sun.
In the process of the Earth's rotation
And revolution around the Sun,
To a person on the surface of the Earth,
The Sun appears to rise from the east of Earth.

That is the apparent. That is the obvious.
Sometimes though,
There is something behind the obvious,
And it can be seen beyond the surface of the Earth.

When you use your mind to orbit
Around the Sun and the planet Earth,
And see both at once together,
You'll see the relationship of one to the other.
You will see a different perspective
When seeing things through a holistic approach.

Prayer of Saint Francis of Assisi

At the end of the day let us pray
the prayer of St. Francis, who may be a Catholic,
but whose prayer is universal, centered on love of God,
<u>and radiating with love of the people.</u>

Lord,
make me an instrument of your peace.

Where there is hatred, let me sow love;
Where there is injury, pardon;
Where there is doubt, faith;
Where there is despair, hope;
Where there is darkness, light; and
Where there is sadness, joy.

O Divine Master,
grant that I may not so much seek
To be consoled as to console;
To be understood as to understand;
To be loved as to love;
For it is in giving that we receive;
It is in pardoning that we are pardoned;
And it is in dying that we are born
To eternal life.

www.ingramcontent.com/pod-product-compliance
Lightning Source LLC
Chambersburg PA
CBHW051544120626
46551CB00013B/1366